Stronger than the Master

Poems of manipulation and escape

Lauren Geertsen

Stronger than the Master
Poems of manipulation and escape
By Lauren Geertsen

Published by Soul Words LLC

Geertsen, Lauren.
1st Edition
ISBN: 978-1979732765

All Photos by Sarah Landa
Cover Design by Shayna McDowell
Proofread by Angela Jooste and Joyce LeBlanc
Edited by Kate Grey and Angela Jooste

To contact the author, please visit LaurenGeertsen.com

TABLE OF CONTENTS

DEDICATION

For my sisters.
Let us speak up together.

Going In

Soul, take thy risk.
Emily Dickinson

PROLOGUE

A well in me breaks open
and suddenly I'm drenched in joy.

I feel the vibrations of an oncoming train
still out of sight:
the person for whom I've waited
will soon appear to me.

An invisible sun
a few feet above my right shoulder
beams down at me.

My whole body is saying,
Thank You Thank You.

I find myself speaking
the language that created me.

KUNDALINI

The light comes upon me like the rumble
of a thousand bumble bees in my hands,
my arms and legs.

I am on your couch,
with you next to me,
when overtaken by this
radiant energy.

This music going through me,
I know
I am the strings
and you are the bow.

Your face tells me
you are watching magic,
This looks like ecstasy, you whisper.

Now, I have a word for the light
splitting open my spine.

The universe has leaped
through me, or I through it.

I open my eyes to find yours,
and discover
I already know you.

REUNION

You are the relief of a familiar face
in a room full of strangers.

WORK

I would not have believed it,
had I heard it,
this simple secret to life:
the person for whom my body asks
will show me
my earth work.

REMEMBERING

The first time our eyes met,
all else went quiet
except the voice
in me saying,
Don't let go.

This is how it feels
when my soul meets
a person it already knows.

With one look I am recognized,
and opened to myself
I find nothing for which to atone.

CONSEQUENCE

The price of holding your hand
that night you walked me to my car
was that our palms fit together
like the two parts of a heart beat.

LANGUAGE

Ann Sullivan took the young hand
of Helen Keller,
plunged it under the cold faucet,
and formed with those fingers
the word
water,
water.

When you first held my hand,
meaning flowed down me
in rivulets and the language
of my body
signed to me
water,
water,

life.

In that moment, Helen understood
not the word itself,
but its significance.

CALL

Come with me into the destruction of love!
I called,
and flung any impediments
to our love out the window:
my religion
my identity
my life.

Please, come!
I called,
but you stayed behind.

CHOICE

I was everything you
ever wanted,
at the price of everything
you had to give up.

RELIGION

Imagine John the Baptist,
the rangy mountain man,
sanctifying souls
in unhallowed river water.

Who told him he could press
into people this indelible blessing?
Not the Church,
but the Divine appointment
of self-realization.

The rite of Baptism says
it is no sin
to remember who you are.

That's why I did a holy thing,
running my tongue down
the pillar of your body.

DETAIL

How it felt
to plunge my breasts
into hands that were
infinitely off limits:

It felt like my heart reached
the high note.

Your touch sang my body alive,
although my soul gave a little shudder.

It knew you were the doors
to freedom,
but also the walls.

SOUL

When I tried to tell you
of your soul, and mine,
you said God was stuck in my mind
like a stain from all that blessed wine
I drank to choke down sick doctrine.

You do not believe in the soul,
only in survival.

But when I retched up the dogma
of my youth to make room for a love
closer to truth —
and that was my love for you —
that was more than survival.

We have placed our hearts,
belly up and full of blood,
on the stone cold altar of this world.

Together we have cried
the tears that are the holy water
of the human race,
we all take a turn
and we all take a taste.

We hold to this earth because we love
enough to live.

Survival is a cheaper explanation
than God.

HEART

You asked me,
What is it like in that beautiful head?

An invitation to truth-telling
I had received only
in my fairy tale life.

I watched my broken pieces
come to know themselves
as my heart.

So that, once whole,
it could hurt even more.

STRAIN

Really?
To be pulled in different
directions by
my soul
and my soulmate?

HIDDEN

My love for you was the sun
shining out of me.

Your love for me was a black cloak
over my body.

You offered me a closet:
your bedroom three nights a week,
and occasionally dinner out,
if I pretended to be your niece.

At 21, I was not yet myself,
and therefore available
to being hidden.

WEIGHT

It's not that the keeping
of secrets is always
bad
but that it is always
heavy.

BLIND

When you say
You are not loving me,

you are saying,
You are not loving me
the way I want to be loved.

Because the way I loved you,
I was not tending to your wounds,
I was asking you to heal.

Love is in the eye
of the beholder,
and you are not
beholding my full love.

GROWTH

You said
I broke your trust.
But how was
I to expand
the box
that contained us
without shattering it?

RESPONSIBILITY

You wanted me to love you enough
so that you would feel whole
even though the poison
of your secrets
remained inside of you.

I gave you all of my love,
forgetting to leave enough
for myself.

STRENGTH

A breakthrough is waiting for you
on the other side of
feeling.

COURAGE

You wouldn't be asked
to feel it all
if you couldn't bear it.

Your heart is stronger
than you.

DISASTER

When you do not know your own power
you try to find it outside of yourself.

STUCK

You live in the past
where the hurts are
familiar.

SOAR

I am angry with your wounds.
I want to trust the love
but you say,
What is love but
being lifted higher
to fall further
and break harder?

My heart says,
I have found the way to fly.

THE ONE

I couldn't have
found myself
without you.

CHALLENGE

It had to be this hard
and I had to love you
beyond reason
so that I learned how to respect
my own heart.

POLITE

I was taught life
is a game of lying
with a smile.

PATRIARCHY

You expected me to hold
all responsibility for how you feel.
And I expected that of me, too.

I already knew how to walk
on eggshells
wearing high heels.

EARTH

Here I am a castaway
on foreign shores without the oars,
wise men say that's okay.

Because the waves that washed
my life to you
give us breath and death too,

and life has love they say.

BOUND

When I convinced myself
it was better to be chosen
than to choose.

When I convinced myself
I had to sacrifice
freedom for love.

PREPARATION

I was well practiced
in the obedience of belief
after all those teachers
and preachers
who told me the truth
and even though I thought
   if that is truth, I don't like God
   if that is truth, I don't want to live
I still believed.

REVELATION

Prayer changes one's
sight of the world
not the state of the world.
True prayer is a request
to change oneself.

Which is why some
consider themselves
highly devout but lack
the courage to pray.

Here's where the rapture got it wrong:
We are not removed from God's green body
when enlightenment comes.
Instead we find ourselves
warm and whole
in the womb of the world.

FOUNDATION

How could you be a home
to me
if you are not one
to yourself?

PAS DE DEUX

When I heard the song *Spiegle im Spiegle*
I was back at age 14,
watching the ballet from the cheap seats,
crying at art for the first time.

I remembered how the violins swelled
and the ballerina placed her fingers
in the palm of her partner's hand.
He held her hand
as one holds a sparrow.

As she leaned closer, he took her waist
and raised her to heaven.
When he floated her down, I saw
her toes kiss the ground
one by one.

I thought, *In this life*
let us set each other down
that tenderly.

And I realized
you have never treated me that way.

GRIEF

I am crying for all the ways I love you
and all the ways it is hard to.

FUTILE

Please,
I said,
do not let me
outgrow our love.

COURAGE

The way I love
is the bravest thing I do.

GONE

You can live your life
in your wounds
but it won't be
with me.

LEGENDARY

When I fell in love with you
I thought,
This is the greatest love story I will ever live.

Then, I fell in love with my soul.

Waking Up

It's better for the heart to break than not to break.
Mary Oliver

AGREEMENT

I imagine the parting scene
before we came to earth.
You said,
I will break my heart for you.
I said,
I will do the same.

DONE

My ultimatum came
when I decided I would not make
my life smaller for you.

NAIVE

Why did I think
I was different enough
than all the women before me?
You were still the same.

CRUCIFIXION

Teach me how to pray,
I asked my soul
and it said,
Take me to the healing.

Afraid, I cried out,
This fate, I do not want it!

Jesus prayed that way,
before the cross.

SAVIOR

I lacked the wisdom
that comes with age.
What saved me
was the wisdom
that comes with writing.

INTUITION

I write to put into words
what my body knows
without words:
to know
what I already feel.

GASLIGHT

My heart told me of a world
bigger than you,
with breathing room
to speak my life.

But you said I could not
trust my heart
to know reality.

You told me to believe in you,
since you were older and wiser
than my heart.

SURRENDER

Slowly and after much pain,
I realize love requires
no force upon the other,
but instead the forgiveness
of the expectations
we have forced upon the other.

There is only what we knew all along:
love,
and our resistance to it.

LEAVING

Now I get it.
I am never at the mercy
of whom my soul loves.

OPENING

It started with the
little voice in me
saying,
No —
This is not my life.

Upon hearing this whisper,
I leaned into myself,
bending my ear to my
invisible mouth.

Then the voice roared
from my belly,
Get out of my way!

and I knew
it meant you.

FEELING

The night I left you
I left crying, wondering
How will I live?
then I realized —
this is living.

Just when I think
I cannot breathe
another breath
under the weight of this world
my soul tells me,
Live the hurt.
It will scald your heart
with beauty.

ANGER

I tried to hold it in
so it didn't hurt you,
but it pulled me in upon myself
and would have continued
until I was gone.

WHITE KNIGHT

I used to believe
you saved me.
Finding me broken
and lonely,
you kissed all the parts of me
I didn't know were beautiful.

Now, I realize my salvation
wasn't you,
but my own love for you.

All along, I held enough love
to save myself.

CONFIDENCE

When I came to know myself
you said I reeked of self-satisfaction.
Too happy with myself
and my work.

That is why, unlike me,
you do not worship
the night sky,
and the trees.

OFTEN

Love hurts.

It is a hazard
of this earth.

BRAVE

When I learned how to love myself,
I stopped waiting for the world
to do it for me.
It is my responsibility.

CONFIRMED

The strongest thing I ever did
was leaving you when I didn't know why.

Then I learned the deception.

My intuition is smarter
than your lies.

FOREIGN

For you,
the pain of your betrayals is
old and practiced.

You brought your lifeboat,
which is waterproof
to my tears.

But I didn't know
pain could feel this fresh.

VIRGIN

Before you, I believed
my love
and my body
were too precious
to be treated this way.

INTRODUCTION

First kiss, first touch, first night sharing a bed,
first morning-after glow, first breakfast together,
first *one more time before you go*,
first kitchen dance partner,
first at-home movie date,
first guitarist to my singing,
first phone always ringing.

First *I love you*,
first *I love you too*.

First betrayal, and the second,
third, fourth, and fifth,
all discovered in a week.

First *I believed what you said!*
first *Stop playing games with my head!*
first can't even eat,
first have to write
instead of sleep.

CHEATING

When I learned your deception,
I wrote these poems and taped them
to your walls.

My words will echo in your house
forever.

This is the part of me
you get to keep.

LOAN

When I learned you said the same
sweet somethings
to the other women,
while we were together,
you took away from me
what I thought I'd have
forever.

MARRIAGE

I was married to the illusion of you.
So were you.
Which is why you never wanted
to marry me.

TIME

Almost three years.
How long it took me to realize
that the truth of me
could not tolerate
the facade of you.

VAMPIRE

You drank my love.
You watched my flesh wither,
and the color leave my face.
And still,
you drank.

NEVER MIND

Those things you said,
about my beauty and my worthiness,
I don't need them after all.
You are not the ground
upon which I stand.

POSSESSION

Your sexuality melted me
like the rest of them.
Sex like that is not love
but skill.

When someone believes they own you
the sex feels like it.

Maybe I could have heard it,
if someone told me
sex is not love.

But the problem was
I wanted love.

UNBOUND

When I absolved myself of responsibility
for your interpretation of me.
When I disowned your eyes.

My value of your opinion
is now as low as your opinion of me.

PSYCHOPATH

You are the kind of smooth
that only comes with practice.

I unwind the thread of my love
to find at the center
not your heart
but the spool of your seduction.

ALONE

You said I would leave you anyway,
being so much younger
and never reasonably content
with your propensity for deception.

I left you,
but you fulfilled your own prophecy.

Leave me out of it.

BLACK MAGIC

I find the tendrils of your energy
in my skin, under my fingernails,
clutching my heart.
I am extracting the darkness,
unraveling myself.

ABUSIVE

Your wounds have teeth.

MISOGYNIST

You see my body as
disposable,
interchangeable,
conquered.

This isn't the way you treat
someone you love,
but someone you hate.

LESSON

You said I had to lie to be loved,
and being loved for the lie of myself
is the closest I'll get to being loved.

That's just how the world is,
you said.

Then I learned
I can always reject the words
which come before someone says,
That's just how the world is.

MIDST

Even in the earthquake of it all,
I keep my heart open.
So the words can come out.

DEVOTED

Was all my love
sucked into
the black hole of you?

Maybe.

But still I believe:
Love is never wasted.

REVENGE

All this flaming hot
gratitude.
Because now I'm free
for the love that is ready
for me.

MINE

Who owns your secrets
If I am one of them?

WRITTEN

You ensnared a woman
who saves her life
with a pen.
How could you not expect
to be put on paper?

HORIZON

If my love was the fire
and I was the phoenix

are you the ashes?

I brush away the dust
and step into my new life,
gleaming in the afterglow.

PROPHESY

I always knew our love
was meant to be shared.

ARTEMIS

I will tell my sisters,
the ones who come after me,
what you did to me.

Speaking Out

When a woman tells the truth she is creating the
possibility of more truth around her.

Adrienne Rich

PERSPECTIVE

Back then, I would have said:
Sisters, break the rules for the person
your soul loves.
Go.

Now I say:
Sisters, sometimes your soul loves
the person who can break it.
Leave.

SELF-PORTRAIT

I stand in the line of fire
praying to catch a bullet
in my heart,
and die to something
I know is real.

FORWARD

Now I know
the pain of denying my soul
is greater than the pain
of destroying my life.

RELIEF

I, the one
with the truth,
always have more power
than the liar.

FACT

There is light, and there is darkness.

You swallowed me into your darkness
and I had to light my way out.

Now, I am so bright
your secrets
have nowhere to hide.

REVOLUTION

Maybe it happened because
I didn't hear it from the other women.
So I will tell the other women.

SHADOW

After I learned to speak
the language of the body,
which is the language of all
beings and beasts,
I spoke to his ghost.

It sounded so like his fear,
I couldn't tell them apart.

It said to me
He needs me, I cannot leave.

He never did give up his ghost,
because he didn't want to walk
alone.

SUGGESTION

I would say to the young woman
who is new to the world:

Just because he is a good lover
doesn't mean he knows how
to love you.

MEDICINE

The truer I tell my story
the more it can be their story.
My sisters will not be as alone
as I was,
and that is the healing.

VOICES

I believed,
for a time,
my life was
not mine to speak.

Now I write my life
and hear the old
whispers saying,
It is not yours to write.

UNSTOPPABLE

I am the weight of all
my life before me,
and all the women with me.

TANTRUM

My sisters,
when it happens the first time,
it is not the first time.

He has already grabbed
another woman that way,
and yelled that loudly at her.
He has been, before, the large man
throwing large items
across the living room.

You may make excuses.
It's because he's hurting.
He still loves me.
Everyone else left him for this, I won't.

Do not be the martyr who enables his cruelty.

Your love hasn't changed him.
The only hope
is that your leaving him will.

Remember this when
the old body longing
wakes up in your bones,
and you reach for the phone
ready to call a mistake.

When a scorpion stings you once,
never invite it back into your bed.

MANIPULATION

Sisters, the predators
will try to convince you
they are not their actions.
They are deeper than that,
or that wounded, they insist.

No.

Their actions are the
truth of them.

SENSATION

Sisters, ask yourself
What does love feel like?

Love can be a hurricane,
or the closing of a door.

Love can be the smallest step
away from the responsibilities
of other people's secrets.

Love can feel like jumping off a cliff,
and landing in a thousand pieces.
Love can be gathering up those pieces
in your arms and deciding all parts of you
are worthy to bring with you.

Love can be taking the last lifeboat from the Titanic,
and watching your life sink behind you.
Love can be running to catch the last bus out of town,
and hearing the screams behind you saying,
You do not deserve freedom for we are not free!

Love is rarely what you expect
but always familiar enough
to recognize.

RECONSTRUCTION

You do not need to be sweet,
my sisters,
kind, but not sweet.
How do you ever make a life you want
being sweet?
Truth is your greater kindness.

PEACE

I just get stronger.
By that I mean softer,
because now I trust
the truth
to take care of me.

VULNERABLE

Yes,
I was in love with my abuser,
for my culture taught me
to love that which hurts me.

Also, there was the soul love
it could not train out of me.

ARTIST

It feels like the skin of my soul is too thin
and though it hurts, I wouldn't change it.
How else would I know the meaning
this world holds?

INDEPENDENCE

I have chosen the
excursion of truth,
not obedience.

IMMENSE

The responsibility to hold him
accountable.

I am the one who becomes
stronger than the master.

TEACHER

She came to me one night, silently,
when I closed my eyes,
and showed me how anger is a force of love.

Who are you? I asked.
She said, *I am a teacher.*

A teacher of what? I asked.
She said, *I am The Teacher of Destruction.*

We went to a cliff-rimmed beach and,
standing in the gray mist,
she cast the sea upon itself
so it crushed a ship without mercy.

Then she took me to the temple,
I watched Jesus turn over the tables
without mercy.

Can I feel you? I asked her
and into me poured the sea.

I opened my eyes and wrote quickly:
I have ships to sink, fearlessly,
so I can love the world unfettered.

INEVITABLE

I will burn down his Rome.
Has he forgotten
I have been taught
by the Teacher of Destruction?

BYSTANDERS

When I tell them
and they say,
I never saw him do that.
You're being dramatic.
That's only your story.

Well.
My story is enough for me.
My story is enough for the world.

EXCUSES

There are many who still find his charm
more convincing than the truth.

They ask me,
But didn't you consent?

As if I must own his responsibility
because I said yes to the sex.

As if the prey must take all responsibility
when caught by the predator.

INSTITUTION

When I was with him
it was always my fault.
Now I speak my story,
and am told the same.

As within,
so without.

CONFUSION

Those who knew him
only as he wished to be known
ask me,
Why do you seek vengeance?

I reply, *Wrong question.*
I seek truth, not vengeance.
Why are you so afraid of
truth
that you will not even
call it by its name?

NEXT

It's hard to love again,
after something like that,
they say.

But I do not fear
that which shows me
my life.

GOOD

Now a stronger man
can take my hand
and hold on for the ride.

DESIRE

I was one who lived by
someone else's fears.

I was not the woman I am now.
One who knows
what she wants
is important,
is necessary, actually,
to the world.

REVEAL

This week, I saw many women
with scars on their arms.
Scars like the smallest sand dunes,
like geometric carvings,
like rites of passage.

Like reminders they are alive,
reminders they wanted to die.

Scars that prove they are
part of the human tribe.
Scars that mark the site
where they tried to excavate
the pain from their heart.

Scars like the battleground that became
the blessed burial ground.

Scars which show the broken places
made stronger.

I want to kiss those scars
like Mary kissed the feet of Jesus,
because I have scars too,
just more hidden.

ENOUGH

You are practiced enough
in the grief of self-denial, my sisters.

Take yourself back into your arms,
be all the tenderness you ever needed.

In caring for your soul,
attend only to what makes it most alive.

FEMINIST

A woman who lives
well-adjusted to her soul.

IMPLORE

Sisters,
I say,
Do not sell your soul
for your soulmate.
But if you do,
earning it back
is the most important
work of your life.

HEALING

There is more.
I will write so much more.
Get ready for the avalanche
of my truth.

About Lauren Geertsen

Lauren began the website EmpoweredSustenance.com at age 19, after using nutrition to heal her autoimmune disease. Five years later, Empowered Sustenance has supported over 35 million people with recipes and resources for holistic wellness. Lauren has written two Amazon bestsellers, *Quit PMS: End Your Menstrual Misery Naturally* and *Quit Acne: The Nutritional Approach for Clear Skin*. Lauren's next book, expected in 2018, will help women trust their bodies and access their intuition.

ACKNOWLEDGEMENTS

I'm deeply grateful to the women who collaborated with me to create this book: Angela Jooste for her editing and proofreading, Joyce LeBlanc for her proofreading, Kate Grey for her coaching, Joy Geertsen for her feedback, Sarah Landa for her photography, and Shayna McDowell for her graphic design. Also, my gratitude goes out to Nina Torres, for her life-changing guidance and encouragement.

I'm grateful for Martha Beck and Elizabeth Gilbert, whose work and workshops inspired me to my way into the light.

Made in the USA
San Bernardino, CA
02 January 2018